EMBER MUSIC

by the same poet

The Impossible Jigsaw (Peterloo Poets, 1985)

Ember Music

STUART HENSON

PETERLOO POETS

First published in 1994
by Peterloo Poets
2 Kelly Gardens, Calstock, Cornwall PL18 9SA, U.K.

**A catalogue record for this book is available
from the British Library**

ISBN 1-871471-41-9

Printed in Great Britain by
Latimer Trend & Company Ltd, Plymouth

ACKNOWLEDGEMENTS are due to the editors of the following journals and anthologies: *Argo, Critical Survey, Cumberland Poetry Review* (U.S.A.), *Encounter, Footnotes, Other Poetry, Outposts, Oxford Magazine, Owl, P.E.N. New Poetry II* (Quartet 1988), *The Poetry Book Society Anthology 1988-1989* (Hutchinson), *Poetry Durham, Poetry Matters, Poetry Now* (B.B.C. Radio 3), *Poetry Review, Poetry Wales, The Rialto, Smiths Knoll, Sparrow* (U.S.A.), *The Spectator, 'Spoils': The Poetry Business Competition Anthology 1991* (Smith/Doorstop), *Staple.*

The poem "Neighbours" was commissioned for the B.B.C. English by Radio series of that title, and broadcast in 1989.

"The Players" was the winner of the Open University Poets Open Poetry Competition 1990.

"The Lost Boys" was a prizewinner in the City of Cardiff Festival Competition '92, and "Elegy for an Old Carpet" won 2nd prize in the Peterloo Open Poetry Competition 1992.

Contents

EMBER MUSIC

The Music of Water

In the beginning this was the first sound:
After the rush of chaos, sudden calm,
The stones in their places, waiting, the warm
Light splashing and dappling shapes on the ground.
Then issues from the womb of time a drowned
Boy surfacing: the first and naked Adam,
His lips gummed, his tongue thick, grunting a psalm
To Earth that aches about him like a wound.

Until he stops and cocks his ear to listen.
A stream, trickling and talking to his thirst,
And teaching him to speak in words that glisten,
Turn, drop, like water as it swells and bursts
On a thorn in the sun. And he is risen
Now, a man. Ready to fall and be cursed.

The Players

Out of the green graves or the road's dust
the dusk assembles them, wisest and least,
like shadows gathered to a feast,
and one by one in candle-fall they come
about the chestnuts and the tombs,
speaking their dumb discourse to leaf,
to stone, and to the sun that lingers
low on the hill where the hay lies mown.

Gargoyles that once were angels hang and grin.
Above the sunken lane the dead lean in.
All the quick world is spring and listening
at time's conventicle, a ring
where thin grey fingers pluck at strings
that resonate through bird-light,
bat-light, half-light, out on the air,
on the dim concentric circles of the night.

Their text, their eloquence, begins to be
our understanding too and our intelligence
is rhymed to theirs and hears as if the trees
translated us; but what they say's grown
brown with lichens, rain-washed, worn away.
Their day has travelled with its dusty sun
and goes ahead, and if we follow them we know
we should become them finally and not return.

For once these players might have been
priest, poet, teacher, physician ...
But now the leather on their heels
is wearing thin. Their eyes see through us
and they're gone, beyond our hearing,
down the drift road where time and timeless join,
turning their pocket-silver twice for luck,
for a moon like the edge of a new coin.

The Newly-weds

For a week they have woken laughing and late
with white planes of sunlight strewn on the bed
and a clean sense of themselves
defined by another's touch.
The world has amused itself by itself:
it has left them alone with a coy smile
to discover the strength of their limbs' love.

And now it comes back with the noise
of churns, with a rollicking truck,
with the farmer's wife who has knocked
to see if they need her to bake
for the journey back. Her flowers
on the sill have begun to drop
but the daffodil light in the room is sweet.

They go down. Their breakfast, a sacrament:
they make eggs with herbs and the toast
burnt black. They wash and they splash
at the pump in the yard
like a pair of birds in a summer bath:
she swings on the squeaking iron arm;
the cup of his hands overflows — and they laugh.

✳ ✳

She wears the dress of her Going Away
to come home — soft crumpled and warm
from the seat of the car. They unload,
numbed with the journey's gloom,
the cases, her hat, his camera.
The steps to the flat are moist with dust
and the pollen scent of afternoon rain.

She changes and sighs and slides into jeans;
(the wardrobe dark in the small room)
in the kitchen he sniffs for a gas leak;
(the pert blue flames bubble up in a crown)
new mugs are unpacked and swung on their hooks;
a host of objects begins to assume
the authority of the day-to-day.

Here are things that will keep them company
for the rest of time — some they chose,
and the presents not to their taste.
The record he slips on the stereo is the past —
from another life, like the soot in the grate.
They sit by the hearth in her mother's chairs
feeling oddly face-to-face.

Moth and Rust

Ah, moth and rust! And falling dust
and the creeping damp that seeps
through brick and lime to the last shelf
and violates each leaf the hand lifts.
They pay no heed of printer's grace-note
space, ink's trace, line's melody.
They are decay's executors:
grey-faced they gather in the library.

We have a box, a cardboard box.
It was your stock of memory,
or part of it: the books
you took down carefully,
replaced in their familiar ranks,
and promised us. Our thanks
are meaningless: the worse for prized
works cast aside, too drab to keep.

The standard lamp and the worn chair,
the spines' picket, all are set steep
on the edge of a roomless deep.
Our books fade with us as we age.
Should you return in time to find
this flower you pressed once
into the page of a summer day,
would you not weep?

In the Museum

After those years he thought it was all over;
A new wife, her family and children
(How oddly grief can take root in the heart)
A day's outing, McDonald's, the Museum ...
Then just one image in a gallery —
A hare strung up and bleeding from the nose —
And he was there again on the black road
Driving his anger at the wall of night.

Each time he left and wasn't going back
The darkness might as well have been a cliff,
The road a chute into eternity,
But slowly as the pain ran out he'd stop
And sleep against the wheel until the dawn
Drew out its horizontal line above
The downs or woke him with its wan rose-wash
In a cold car park looking out to sea.

Only the once he knew it was the end:
The night the half-crazed creature leaped across
His tunnel of white halogen and swerved
And kicked and struck against the number-plate,
A dull thump, hopeless, though he stopped to search
And found her lying on her folded bones.
(If you could run time back what's done and said
might be reversed, those accidents disproved.)

A painter's hare bought at some butcher's slab,
Immortalised in oils. Cook took it then —
Convenient; no carcass; no regrets;
Simply the picture hanging in its frame ...
And now young voices crowded in the room
Tug at his sleeve and call, repeat his name,
Urgent, anxious that he should catch them up —
As if time lost might somehow be regained.

15

Neighbours

These two were neighbours fifty years,
who leaned across the new wire fence
in 1943 and joked and frowned at whitefly
in the cabbages. They'd wipe their brows;
one spoke, one laughed, admired the rows —
first flowering of the Dig for Victory.

An age then of spare utility: the flat
square bungalows with geometric frames
that sprouted on the field-edge overnight,
that in a month were homes and lives,
not rich but busy, and not blighted yet
but pinched with a war austerity.

Clear afternoons they'd push back from their spades
and watch the sky grow black with Fortresses
turning and droning like a hive of bees
put up to swarm and settle on Berlin.
Then shadows flitted on the mind of nights
to come, in wet tin shelters, cowering.

And yet, they say, these two old men
who sit and gaze out from their bench
half drowsy with the sun and age,
those were the days, the good old days,
when families next door sat round a lamp,
sang worn-out songs to drown the raids.

Reels, reels of memory, of VE Day: a whole street
drunk in each others' arms on nothing more
than pure relief. All this and then
decades of peace: the century unwinding
on a slow downhill from ration-book to pension-book,
and illnesses, and the gardens left to weeds.

These two were neighbours fifty years:
their houses were a temporary affair
that lingered after skies had cleared
and the world spun on. Yet still at night
their lighted window-squares share one black roof,
fixed by the small sharp nail-heads of stars.

Sketching on the Underground

But for the slightest movement of his head,
the eyes' flit, lighting and up again—
that and the pen's quick tremors at the pad,
hid in the rocking motion of the train ...

This is his way—to pay the unposed
moment his attentions, to eschew the vain,
and what the world would call remarkable,
seeking instead the self-possessed.

The woman is too much alone in thought
to be aware of him at all, and she suspects
only the window and her greying hair.
He knows this is the last true test
of art—to break time's fall.

She will be gone in one stop, or the next.

Late Train

These carriages have plied their trade all day
in the to-fro heat from King's Cross up to
Peterborough; minute by airless minute
in their net of steel and high wire: the shimmer
on the parallel, throb of the power car —
continuous shrinking to a vanishing-point,
an always-coming, always-getting-there.
And now in the cool night, the vents open
and sucking in the still-warm smells, oily,
unwholesome and evocative, they reel
once more, and I leaf through a book, recall
a man in winter clothes waist-deep in grass
who gathered lupins in the wilderness
between the slow-line and the dead canal;
the house-backs and the businesses, the yards;
the curious legend 'May Be Tamped' in rough
block letters on a bridge; and the number
CHAncery 8800, the ghost-phone
of an office-cleaning company, preserved
above graffiti-reach on a warehouse wall.
Now, in the late train, no-one needs to talk,
and at the stops no voice disturbs or shouts
until the sudden bleeping of the doors
announces motion and restores the pulse
that nods these journey-makers on the breast
of sleep and soothes their day-won statuses.
The woman opposite is fair, full-limbed,
and of an age that's done with innocence.
About my age. But still that unselfconscious
rag-doll falling of her head's pure childhood.
Sleep takes us like a mother to her trust.
And as my thought goes straggling at that edge,
I dream of Patsy Toseland and Rosemary,
and Cheryl Dant: the girls who held my hand
on the first day of school in the big land
beyond the garden of my first five years,

or naturally were generous and teased
me with a smile or the promise of a kiss.
The late train rocks these random passengers
till they become all whom I have forgotten
but knew once. Souls journeying by chance,
I muse how you might be asleep somewhere
like this and travelling the spinning night
on other trains to other towns and yet
all drawn down lines of time's discovered map
darkly towards some island of the blessed.

The Price

Sometimes it catches when the fumes rise up
among the throbbing lights of cars, or as
you look away to dodge eye-contact with
your own reflection in the carriage-glass;
or in a waiting-room a face reminds you
that the colour supplements have lied
and some have pleasure and some pay the price.
Then all the small securities you built
about your house, your desk, your calendar
are blown like straws; and momentarily,
as if a scent of ivy or the earth
had opened up a childhood door, you pause,
to take the measure of what might have been
against the kind of life you settled for.

A Souvenir

A fortnight's milk gone rancid on the step,
no answer at the stair,
they found him peacefully in bed
with ancient beer-stains on the sheets
and twelve brown bottles round the floor.

He'd spent his wealth — good land
sold off, prize cattle gone.
Not worth the search: the mattress
stuffed with old newsprint,
pillows with nothing more than down.

They stripped them off and there — the bomb
crusted and barnacled alive with rust,
corroded tench of dog-eared fins,
a dent across the casing where
the trawling ploughshare forced it up.

You see him stoop, caress the shape
and clutch it to him in his arms,
a drunkard's trophy cradled home
to share the silence of his room
before these strangers came with quiet hands.

Too like a corpse they ease it now
behind the whispers and the blinds.
Bird-chatter hushed, the still air waits —
a one-gun eighty-pound salute,
and sods of pasture slopping in the pond.

Girl with a Cat

(after the painting by Pierre-Auguste Renoir, 1880)

It is morning in the *Rue Cortot*,
warm morning; the sunlight crumbles the walls
like bread and the dust falls
in the window's eye and delights
with its touch the surface of things.
There are bees in the garden,
the dew is gone. A grey dappled cat
lies asleep in the quoin of the roof
and below in the courtyard
an old woman sings.

Angèle, how you prattle — of nothing,
of lives, of the warmth of the sun,
but you can't sit still
and your dark lids droop
and the picture that *Monsieur Renoir*
has begun is nothing — no good.
You are young; you must sleep
you have love on your side
and your pert young face is your fortune
though not for long.

In the courtyard the woman is feeding the cat;
it curls round her feet with its fur
like smoke. It purrs and it arches
and dips at the milk. The painter leans out
with his hands on the sill. The garden
is full of the light of poppies and daisies,
shade-alleys of grasses and speechless leaves ...
but the frame of the window
is suddenly empty — Renoir is descending
the staircase in leaps.

She is young; she must sleep;
her heart's hopes are simple; her face is her fortune
though not for long. And *Monsieur Renoir*
has begun again in his *grande affaire*
with the surface of things.
It is morning in the *Rue Cortot,*
warm morning; from the courtyard below
the smell of bread baking.
The cat shuts its eyes in the street-girl's lap
and the painter smiles and his brushes sing.

The Lost Boys (studio photograph, 1898)

'Those frank eyes where deep I see
An angelic gravity'
(Matthew Arnold: *A Memory-Picture*)

At two years old your sister is too young
To invent the future: she sits intent,
Absorbed in some small thinking of her own.
But you, in button-waisted Norfolk suits,
Breeches, sharp new white collars, handkerchiefs,
What griefs beyond the camera's eye begin
To cloud gazes like yours? Is that the cause,
The portrait photograph lodged at your feet —
Of your brother, Clement, dead aged seven,
Haunting you then as it might haunt us now,
Lost behind glass, wistful and far away?
(Yet he was safe from all but sunlight's slow
Decay.) Is it the camera's black pall?
Or maybe in the lens's kaleidoscope
You see the tumbling century ahead
Fall and re-shape itself into a war
Whose odds will take one of the three of you:
Rupert, who drew, was fine and sensitive
And married young; Wilfrid, astute, canny,
Quick to make fun, of art and bookishness;
Or Julian whose studies took him on
To university and schoolteaching —
Arnold and Tennyson, the pregnant lines
For we are all, like swimmers in the sea,
Poised on the top of a huge wave of fate,
Which hangs uncertain to which side to fall.
Well, fate's wave, duly, as you knew it would,
Crashed and went sprawling up the beach of time,
And left the image of the moment there
When you were posed together in the frame
Knowing somehow that this was serious,
That childhood was a grave and separate thing,

Solemn like church, profound, soon to be gone.
Outside the studio the afternoon
Was bright and sharp, and the shops were open;
The horse-drawn trams were rattling down the street.
Somebody in an office by the docks
Was totalling a ledger; someone else
Was checking with the Harbour Master's clock
To make sure that his boat would catch the tide.
The World. Pride and Responsibility.
And destiny, which you stepped out to meet.

A Postcard to John Greening

The long, empty perspective of the beach
At dusk, the tide-line ragged, the odd gull
Mewing, alone, far out across the reaches
Of silt that merge invisibly with the swell;
The green salt smell of the pools, the oily
Detritus and the tell-tale tracks of man
And boy—all that accumulates, slowly,
Washed up on the mind's receptive strand;
These are our keepsakes, wispy souvenirs
For the year inland where things are hard-edged
And the wind forgets its promises: the clear
Uncomplicated days our childhoods pledged—
To wanderers with nets and spades who planned
Great bridges, ships and mansions in the sand.

Another Country

(After the painting 'Cotswold Blooms' by Adrian Paul Allinson)

It was like this, but never quite like this
sharp-focus garden where the shadows
fall in the bright light perfectly,
where each step, each bush, each gable
and each flower-bed is proof of its own geometry.

Thus Eden was, still in the sun,
with only the bees' hum and the black
cat's tail-twitch, felt of its tongue —
a toad by a wet stone, ants crawling at random.
And so it was when we were young.

Sly, painterly deceit; for even then
this garden was already gone, like scent
of warm days, curled skies, in the womb
of summer, before the combine harvester
and DDT, the private car, the bomb.

Was it a lie then, Allinson, or an ideal
that your mind's eye lit upon?
Nostalgia for an old world, benign,
where death stood further, further off,
and nature would heal us if we gave it time?

It hides now, like a lost key, a talisman,
this house where the last of the lilac is browning
and lilies peal white bells on their stems.
A casement is open, the door to the kitchen ajar.
Your mother's voice is calling for you to come in.

Armada

The water butt is deeper than I am tall,
its rust-fathoms limitless, gold
darkness, flecky, cold and obscure.
I have dragged it here, the chopping-block:
my ships a shard of kindling each,
three nails in a studied tri-mast line.
Bowed card grows soggy, and the sails,
stiff to the model winds,
are yellowing for lack of keel.
These seas are treacherous: their rainbow oils,
their cobwebs, and the gutter spout …
I am a god. I shout thunder;
my hand makes waves, makes the storms roll.
I freighted once a round half-crown,
but my ship was doomed and tipped and drowned.
The coin winked to the honey-depths
like a bounty never, never to be found.

National Savings

Half-a-crown, heavy, something worth having;
It bought a Football Monthly or a bar
Of Cadbury's so thick that when you tore
The foil off it wouldn't break — gleaming
Ingots of chocolate: wealth for the dreaming!
Yet Mondays we exchanged the coin for thin
Blue likenesses, stamps, of Prince Charles: token
Of promises deferred, virtuous saving.

Elsewhere, wise fathers dealt in equities,
Invested at the preferential rates
That claimed their sons cold beds in Marlborough dorms.
And we, the rising meritocracy?
Our booklets of complete certificates
Would scarcely pay our Grammar School uniforms.

Nocturnall

Hardly the year's midnight, but the blank hour
That you wake in and just can't sleep again,
    Too early to be called a dawn:
    February; bitter; the car
        Small on the roads, a toy.
Unfrozen for an afternoon the sky
Has smiled a tight-lipped smile and turned away —
That kind of emptiness. The world's a husk.
Odd street lights flicker, crystal in the dusk.

To drive across the map of scarp and dip —
Rockingham, Uppingham, the sweeping spread
    Of the Vale of Belvoir sprinkled
    With week-old snow — is still to slip
        Back through a melt of words:
These boroughs and these burgesses, these woods
Clinging like balding remnants, and the roads
Asking their way to parishes. All this
A cipher for what England is — or was.

Returning, as you spin between the walls
Of drifts, the shining signs are all you have
    To prove the car has not sheered off
    Into black space, a dud capsule
        Propelled at the future.
You're glad to see another human creature
Reel home from a shuttered pub: his stagger
Proves the earth turns as it always did,
Warmed by the whisky-laughter in his blood.

The spread estates of Corby are alive,
But only just, at 2 a.m. A town's
    Decline: an index of the times.
    Things struggle on; you can survive.
       What made the front page once
Is old-hat now: it's more than four years since
The rocket-gantries of the furnaces
Came down. The fences moved on up the road—
The lamps, security, the all-night glow.

For journey's end, a slow count-down of names,
Worn and familiar: the signposts blink
    Lowick, Titchmarsh, Bythorn, Brington,
    Molesworth, Catworth, Tilbrook … home
      In the brittle frost-dark.
And you pity the fox in the white arc
Light, the police at the gates, their vans parked.
Tomorrow's headlines (but too late to hold):
Young Mother & Two Children Die of Cold.

Vesper, November

The end of the month; the end of the day:
the garden completes its chameleon change
to the browns of decay, the soaking green,
the camouflage of the sunken year.
There are still, you're aware,
those few stray blooms that some hint of sun
has confused into light,
but you know they can't last: sweet peas
on a fence, and the silvering leaves
of the sage, and the periwinkle's blue
slight stars — no more than requests
the condemned heart asked;
and they glow in uncertain dusk
like a prisoner's cigarette.

What else is there left? To resign yourself
to this hard-bitten squad of cold days
marching in? To release regret?
To turn around and to blindfold your eyes
and forget? Let that be enough. Unless,
unless there is one thing to keep,
in the blue of space, in the emptiness
of sky on the roof of the shed:
one final rose that broke out of its bud
too late, that hangs shivering there in the wind
like a girl with no shawl and no coat.

And too high to reach.

And your hand as pure as frost.

The Heron

A servant's soul. He said I had a servant's soul
    and he spat in the grate
and left me crying here like the wretch that I am.
So I thought then I should never touch him again
    and I hated myself
and I sobbed for an hour alone in the cold room.
    I'd had enough. I'd go.
Though the roads were crueller than he, I would walk home.
Then he knocked and came in with the bird in his hands.

He was red — with the heat of straw and horses on him.
But the anger was gone, and his face oddly still.
    I was certain at last
I should never be quite alone; something of him
    stuck with me, a splinter;
something he didn't want to give that remained yet.
    I said, It's a heron.
And he said, Yes, it was dead by the stable door
at the foot of the wall, in the snow, in the drain.

Its eye, he said, was deep as a fish's eye, its
    wing's grey was my cloth dress.
And what kind of help was left for us, when the bird
he had watched a week as it stalked the river's length
    could be driven to this,
to a heap of frozen rag flung down from the roof,
with the rods of its legs furred white in ice, where the
    horses breathed, where the pond
it had poached from in spring was snapped tight like a gin?

The Difference

It's the knave's luck and the poet's trick
to stand in the right place at the right time.
One pockets fortune with a smile;
the other spends it out in rhyme.

I thought this walking in a wood
where, snowbound, nothing stirred
but the odd slipfall of ice from a branch
sprung in my path by a frightened bird.

That frozen day I saw a tree
become a fountain pouring light.
The sun undid the oak's identity
and spilled for ten minutes, seeming endlessly,
what never could be counted, an infinity
of glistered water-splinters in my sight.

The Bee Nativity

Midnight. Christmas night. The clock
strikes and the stroke falls from the tower
in the starry air, like the first beat
beginning the chant, beginning plainsong.
In the garden the six white hives
breathe in, and inaudible, scarcely
audible, like the after-thrum of the bell,
like the honeyed hum of its resonance,
the homage of hundreds of bees has begun.

Their psalm is the joyful noise
of the lands of summer, burdened,
unburdening: the pasture, the clover,
the limes by the long canal and the thistles
lisped by the breeze — that old sentimentalist.
Mellifluous. Melliferous. Their tryst
with sweetness of all that's new-born:
the hay-scented cradle; the blossom;
the child; the midwinter beast-snuffled sun.

Ember Music

The raked-out coals are glowing in the hearth,
Crisp, cokey, light, they jingle on the grate
Like tiny chimes blown by their own last heat.
The chimney draws their music up; its breath
Excites them into flower — flame-petal wreath
To all of day that's fallen through and spent.
The rest is ash, no more than ash; once burnt
It says: each nightfall is a kind of death.

We crouch to warm our hands against the mesh
And listen for the tin-foil threnody.
You call it sleigh-bells distant over ice,
I think of spheres: the way the world turns once
From dawn to darkness in a day; the rest
Is ash, no more than ash, and powdery.

CROYLAND

A Hermit's Journal

(for Kevin Crossley-Holland)

In the seventh century, Croyland (now Crowland, Lincolnshire) was an uninhabited island deep in the inhospitable and undrained fenlands to the north east of Peterborough. St Guthlac was a Mercian warrior before his conversion to Christianity. He entered the monastery at Repton, and after two years was given permission to depart and seek out a hermitage.

The sequence uses details from Felix's Latin *Life of St Guthlac* (edited & translated by Bertram Colgrave, Cambridge University Press, 1956). The versions from the Guthlac poems in the Exeter Book are based on S.A.J. Bradley's prose translations (*Anglo-Saxon Poetry*, Dent, 1982).

1.

The boatman dips his oar
in the sticky waters;
the weed swirls in his wake
and the ripples close.
It begins now,
my apprenticeship to solitude
in this no man's land
of the soil and skies,
where the sun rises and sinks
in marches of fen on every hand.
The four horizons
gather their winds to hurl
the seasons across this place:
a wilderness,
an emptiness, a space
to meet God on his own terms.
I am bound now to search
my path into grace
between these alder groves
these ambiguous shades
with their water-mint
and their poisonous bittersweet.
I am bound
to make it my own,
this trackless island,
sunken in chaos.
My acre of savage Eden
voided of men.

2.

Today, an inventory of beasts:

freshwater fishes, eels, the heron's feeding;
the small amphibians — frogs, toads, newts.

Among the rushes, coot, warblers, grebe
of both kinds; lithe worms; fenny snakes.

When the sun is out, butterflies,
beetles, bugs in abundance.

One common kestrel hangs on its cliff of air
where the grasses beach themselves in waves.

Larvae, thin nymphs with telescopic legs.
The mask of the gauzy dragonfly.

By dusk, moths, bats, glow-worms ...

No demons.   So far.

3.

Who dug my cell?

Thieves.

Where did they sweat?

Down in the ark of a grave.

What were they seeking?

Gold, crystal, garnets and ivory.

What did they find?

Bones in the black soil,
worms, a flask, ivory skulls.

How did they go?

Furtive, fearful, charged
with all ill.

Why did they so —
scraping my cell
with their iron crows,
their hands;
guilty, unknowing?

Working God's will.

4.

Easy enough to disregard the gloss of mirrors:
sickness and hollow age and death.

Too long with these coarse, sore hides on my bones,
today in the lake I caught my own face, shrunk, thinner.

A scrape of barley-bread when the sun's set;
the taste-sense dull, like silt in my bowl.

My head has become a shell of doubt. At night
the dread of the ravening dark, the last threshold.

Time past, too long in lighted rooms, in brazen cups,
drunken and draining desire's lees for the drug lust.

Too many beds with neither then; these lips
stained: blood; kisses; a woman's promises.

Enough! As if it were not enough to have strewn
men out of their homes, set torches at their thatch.

A third of all their pathetic wealth I gave them back,
proud, with that condescending charity.

Each time I look, the glass of my life shows ill.
This cell's not tight enough to squeeze me out of hell.

This suffering itself is another kind of vanity.

5.

How frail the flesh,
the body's bone thermometer,
the thin capillaries
of fingertips and toes
that still record
night's rigor mortis setting in
and the slow thaw by day.
And seasons too—the spirit
flaking out of its almost-death
with the greening earth,
with the fledgling leaves
close-budded in their shells.

April. My face pulls
to the southern sky
for hints of warmth
and the looked-for time
when the swallows come
like a promise reaffirmed.
I slept today
at my open door,
and I dreamt my arms, my knees
my breast aflame with wings.

To wake
and to lift the small birds up
to their place in the eaves!

To nest the storm-blown
pulse of their life
in my hands!

6.

A visitor. A thin young monk
who is much possessed by writing.

Truths, no doubt, of the deepest kind.

Each day between prayers
he sits for an hour
at his sloping desk
with furrowed brow.

No doubt he is sowing thought
in his fertile mind.

Alas, as we knelt today in the oratory
a pair of mad black jackdaws
in at the window
stole up his parchment, flapped it out,
and vanished it to the depths of the mere.

Dark moods! Despair! His text lost!

But the boat is there and I send him off
in the maze of mysterious creeks
to where he may find
the reeds bent with his paper's weight,
and not one word of his wisdom smudged.

An act of fortune, or High Design?
Who can tell?
By God's grace his manuscript
is retrieved from the waters' clutch.

It would seem, then, that he writes well.

7.

Last night, a fever, and then the demons came,
as I knew they would.
But to go to the lip of hell and back —
my soul sickens within me still.

It began with the cracks in the floor
and the wall where they slimed in,
their bodies yellow and soft as phlegm,
and the stench choking the air of the room;
each one with its own foul grin, its slobbered beard,
its skull like the bulbous head of a cretin.

Their knees and their elbows twisted out;
even their bowels were visible
through the slack transparent-ochre skin.
They came with the stink of sin on their breath,
with obscene screams, like the shrieking of calves
in an abattoir.

Then they began their tortures.
I sang: 'The Lord is at my right hand ... '
They drove thorns in my finger-ends,
dragged brambles across the tender zones
of my limbs till I cried aloud.
They thrust my face down in the mere
till my breath burst and I knew I drowned;
they cried: 'Guthlac, leave this place!'
I replied once again:
'The Lord, The Lord is at my right hand.'
They scourged me with cords
knotted with iron butterflies;
they brought machines
from the forge of their sulphur-den
to try me until I swooned into death.

In that dream, the skies were alive
with the buzz of wings. I was borne aloft
on the back of a cloud of their grim kind,
and the black wind, like a locust-storm
transported me north and set me down
on the rim of a great volcano
surging with flame. And it rained there,
in the fire-sea, with bolts of frozen hail.

As I watched, the host of the devil-kind
began to wail: 'O Guthlac, we can cast you in
where the heat of your lusts and your manifold sins
will consume your flesh like wax on the wick
of your bones. Behold, the vents of Erebus,
the burning stones, the boiling Styx,
and the molten gulfs of Acheron!'
I cried in reply: 'Woe unto you, you seed of Cain.
You are no more than dust and ash of a fevered dream.
I am ready. So cast me in if you can!'

And with that the fever began to turn:
I felt in my veins a white calm,
like a drug that salves and dissolves pain,
and my mind was filled with radiance —
the invisible face of the saint whom I loved
and to whom I prayed each night of my fast,
Bartholomew, with his seraph-train, who spoke
one word that drove the crawling demons home.

From that moment on, I sank toward dawn
when the sun with its simple warmth
came touching the walls of my room.

8.

(from Guthlac A)

At once when Bartholomew spoke the God-word,
then Guthlac's spirit swelled in bliss.
All the submissive horde of the Satan-kind
cringed to obey the behest of the saint.
Thus blessed with beneficence, Guthlac began his journey
back to the hallowed-spot thankfully trusting Grace.
Gently, in God-fear, they gathered him up,
anxious for his comfort, and careful to keep him safe.
Home to the holy-place they bore him in triumph,
where the host of birds chorused the wise-man's return
in loud song, as if their voices would burst.
For often the holy sage would hold out food for them
when, hungry, they fluttered about his hands,
fearless and greedy, glad of such aid.
In this way, the gentle soul had withdrawn from the world,
preferring the quiet-counsel and peace of the woods,
delighting instead in the wild-creatures' companionship.
The cell where he struggled was newly sanctified.
Around about, the landscape broke forth in blossom;
the cuckoo spoke with her two notes of spring.
Renewed in resolution, Guthlac could rest in his dwelling-place,
in the green, God-guarded ground of his cell,
where divine strength had driven the devils off.
What purer desire distilled from man's love than this?
Is there any remembered among our fathers,
or such we have known since then ourselves?

9.

A great white owl
with quilted wings like an angel
has made its residence
in the trusses that span my roof.
The brush of its comings and goings
has shadowed my sleep.
When I pray in my cell I always keep
the south door ajar:
the blackbirds, a robin, a coot
will come in and potter
about my feet while I'm still.
The fish, too, will attend my call:
I speak when I go to cast them bread;
then I wait to watch the lake-top boil.

But a price is paid for such
gifts of God; such knowledge
cuts like a two-edged knife.
There are days, more frequently now,
when the strangers arrive
at the landing-place
and the signal rings,
and with slow heart I must go
to answer their visiting.

There are those who journey from monasteries
with their doubts, their curiosity,
who will sit at meat with me
and will judge in their secret hearts
what they see of this old eccentric
who lives out his life in a nest
of timbers lost in the fen.
Again, there are those who are sick
in body or limb who come brave
in the hope that my fasting, my prayers
and my remedies will do more
than all their physicians can.

Today, a young man whose madness
the doctors cannot mend.
There is nothing left to defend his soul
from eternal fires but my faith
and our actions of penitence.
We must go, once again,
to the oratory, to the font,
to the edge of a black abyss
more profound than despair;
and there I must fight three days
or more till the devil breaks.

Each time I am certain,
yet racked with doubt:
I must pull my miracle out
like a conjurer with a great
infallible trick: my devout hands
must take his head, and my words
must banish the beast in his brow
with a God-sweet breath.

His parents will pay the dues of faith.
They may build a church.
Most probably they will broadcast
my name with all favoured speech.
Alas! I have not gone seeking such fame;
but to follow in patient ways
the paths to those truths
that fall with the hush of an owl's wings,
those wisdoms that gather in solitude
like the birds at my feet.

10.

(from Guthlac B)

Often on frost-bound days, forced in by hunger,
the shy bird-flocks flew to feed from his hand
and afterwards remained among the reed-beds,
repaying their sustenance sweetly with song.
And strangers too, the sick, the sorrowful in mind,
would call at his cell for counsel and God's help.
Not one of them whose need had driven him on
to seek out this saintly man on the scene of his temptation
departed despairing of his dark condition,
but each restored, raised by that special power
to health, healed in both body and soul
went forth in praise and prayer and gratitude
while God was pleased to grant him longer days.

But death's disseverance, dawn of attrition's end,
was near at hand for the holy man —
full fifteen years from his first rest in the wilderness.
The Holy Ghost, the Comforter, came down from above,
speaking his benediction to the blessed evangelist
whose breast grew hot and burned with flame,
his soul filled with the fervent need to find its home.
Then sudden sickness silted through his veins,
though Guthlac still maintained his mood of cheerfulness,
and as the illness took fierce hold,
it licked like fire at his bony frame.
This was the bitter cup first brewed for Adam
by Eve and the Devil when Eden fell.
From that time on, for that sin's memory,
no man on Earth could escape or refuse
the deep cup of death at the door of eternity.
Nobody born of flesh, bondman or lord
can fight or fend off its fell advance.
Just so this death, cold and companionless,
drew near to Guthlac now through the dark of night.

One follower remained who daily would attend his cell.
This man was patient, pure in heart,
and sought him in the silence of the sacred hall
that he might hear discourse of heavenly things,
gladly to glean the teachings of the saint.
He found his teacher ill-at-ease and sick,
of a great grief that gnawed him at his heart.
And thus the servant, speaking to his guide:
'How can it be your spirit is so sorely tried?
My friend and master, father, refuge ...
Can you not command words, converse,
comfort my mind?' Blinded by tears
he sought to know how the disease would go with him,
whether indeed the illness would abate.

The saint struggled to muster breath,
enough to answer the anxious man.
'My friend, these limbs grow fiery with pain:
the thief death has the keys of my life
and waits to unlock my body's treasure-house.
I must exchange it soon for a roof of loam,
the earthen walls and floor of the grave.
My soul may seek no more than seven nights' respite:
at the dawn of the eighth day it will ease away,
be freed to receive its benedictions, its rewards,
before God's seat, its journey's end.
My spirit yearns already for unceasing joys.
Now you have knowledge of my body's death.
Its wait was long and tortured in the World.'

A time then of weeping and bleak moods:
the young man's spirit clouded and grew dark,
knowing the saint's impatience to move on.
Although he struggled, sorrow spilt in tears
as he prayed to understand what fate ordained.

✳ ✳

52

The seven days had duly passed
after pain's arrow-shower attacked his lord
and probed with its barbs his heart's fortress
when once again the patient youth
hurried his footsteps to the holy place.
He found the old man prostrate, overwhelmed,
much racked with suffering, his sure hope gone.
The servant's heart was hollow and afraid.
Knowing the end was near, fearful he spoke
words that till now he had not dared to ask:
'Beloved lord, best-favoured of God,
often my mind has troubled me to tell
who it may be that I hear speak with you
each evening when the eager-resting sun
sinks down behind the westward rim
of the flat fen? Father and comforter,
reveal this voice, this visitor's identity,
who speaks with gentleness and great authority,
invisible, yet audible, alone with you.'

After a long pause the pious man
spoke slowly, struggling for breath:
'Listen, my friend, this is a secret
never before broached, betrayed to no-one,
because I was afraid that fools would prattle,
make of it a miracle, marvel and embellish it:
I have no wish to boast or broadcast such a thing,
or cause displeasure to my Lord and risk His wrath.
From the second year, my solitude was blessed
by my Victorious Lord, the Life-giver:
He saw fit to send a celestial angel
who came at dusk each dawn and eventide,
a servant of God, secure in His supremacy,
healing my every hurt, my heart's anxieties,
showing me His will through the gift of Wisdom.
Such wisdom has permitted me intuitively to know
the inmost thoughts and workings of men's minds
when they have come for conference to my cell.

My loyal confidant, for our love's sake,
for the sake of the trust sustained between us
now and always, be answered and be comforted:
I will not leave you languishing alone;
I shall be with you even beyond the grave.'

Then he sank back, head bowed against the wall,
not giving up but fighting still
against the agony of every breath.
It seemed then the sweetest fragrance,
like summer blossom scenting the fields,
spread from his lips and issued forth
the whole day long, continuing and pure.

Across the reeds, the flat wash of the mere,
the sun's path glittered as it sank.
The northern sky, swirling with cloud,
grew dark and overcast, hauling a heavy mist,
and night in its course bore down upon the earth.
Then suddenly a light of all-surpassing brilliance
broke from the heavens above the hermit's cell.
This holy radiance, a noble brightness,
shone all the night about the holy-man,
dissolving shadows in its clarity till dawn
broke in the east across the old sea-path.

Then Guthlac, warrior of God, arose,
ending his wait, pain's harrowing,
and spoke humbly, haloed in light.
'Companion, my friend, the time has come
when you must go and conscientiously discharge
the tasks that I have asked of you.
Carry this message quickly to my sister:
tell her I have begun my journey on
along the road to the gloriousness of God.
I have denied myself her presence in this life
that we might meet matched in perfection
and abiding love before God's throne.
Entrust to her the burial of my corpse
where soulless it may rest in its sandy hill.'

Refreshed by the sacrament he raised his hands
and seemed to see beyond this life,
turning his gaze in rapture up to Heaven.
Then his cold body fell away.
Released, his soul went rising like a lark.

At this the light blazed all about
a bright beacon binding earth and sky,
a holy incandescence like a fiery tower
wherein the angels sang anthems of victory
and saints rejoicing sanctified his path.
Thus was the island filled with ecstasies,
sweetness of air and angel-sound,
transformed, beyond the power of word to tell.
Even the sun, eclipsed, shone dim,
the earth shook and silent nature quaked.

Meanwhile the messenger grew much afraid,
with drained courage hastened to his boat
and launched again across the slate-grey lake.
His wave-steed briskly slipped the water-face,
his sorrow like the swirling depths beneath.

At Crowland

Time tears them down, the abbeys
and the choirs of stone:
slow-motion centuries dissolve
their sandy heads and their saints' bones.

Somewhere across the water-lighted fen
a barn sinks on its holy quoins;
behind this wall a pair of drunken bishops
shoulder-to-shoulder tilt and lean.

Roofless, their pillars rise to loft a firmament
vaulted with cumulus, pricked out in blue.
Where jackdaws rasp and pigeons smothering reply,
here Guthlac keeps his monument alive:
a vast arched window on the sky
that swifts skim screaming through.

BRICKYARD POEMS

(for Katherine)

Planting

My love, in this stone ground
I am forging a green ring:
round our house I shall set a spell
of roots as pale and thin as string —
the blaze of a stake with each,
and a forkful of dung, and a curse
that it cling to the seasons' wheel,
thread down for a grip
on the earth's giving.

My love, in the mixed clays
this spade is carving
fylfots to brave the winds' song:
for cherries' gems and globy crabs
and the alders' shimmering.
What then can man or winter bring
whiter against the birches' bark
to keep my wish from rising?

My love, I have pledged an oak
for its Lammas shoots
a yew for slow growth, for immortality;
and hawthorn they called good hope
and swathed for a marriage-torch:
haga — the hedge,
charm against sorcery.

Venus

When the clocks go back
it's an old world, dusky at five,
with the whiff of that smoky
winter mood in the tops of the hedges,
the banks of low cloud — the shoals
that rest on the hills' rim
where the sun slipped.

As you drive home west
with your headlights dipped
the verges' tufts
become animals, become tufts,
and the sky's blue is fragile,
holy and cold,
where the one star lifts
like an aumbry lamp
in that vault, in that emptiness.

The horizon's pinks go rosy, go dim,
a colour as thin as paraffin.
You crest the hill
and the house below
in its fold of the land
has begun to dissolve —
from its ditches up to its chimney blanks.
It drains its shape down the black earth's sump.

While the planet hangs like a crucifix
of acetylene

on the night's brink.

A Day's Work

Bent backs, curved at the roof-ridge:
driving downhill, I took them first
for two great birds, hunched up there, perching.
The scaffold whistles to the north-east wind.
All day they set a raw geometry of truss and purlin,
the gable's blueprint on the sky, bony, wide-open.

Hand up to hand, the draughtsman's line solidifies.
Tricked out with stars tonight it dreams
of snows, floods — like the half-built Ark.
Below, auspiciously, the angles clipped
from the rafters' ends breathe up their scent
of sawdust-pine, and crack and sputter in the fire.

Cleopatra

The throne she sat on was a stack of blocks
our spattered Ford her nuptial barge —
they roamed at large, ran riggish round
the barn and house: he followed her,
a stepping dance. And she
was proud and loyal and extravagant.
And her eye was dark as beady glass.

Ask, Where's the Queen?
Speak softly ... and then say
the speed of some young Caesar
marked her life. Ah, she was wife
to more than car and bank account!
But greed's metallic lusts strike out:
the roar she understood too late was
'Progress!' the great obscene mob-shout —
prestige in horse-power, gloss success.
And down that steep the world goes headlong
to destroy its loveliness.

Your crown's awry.
I'll mend it ... and lay by
this cloth-of-gold, the fine limp neck.
That peacock's flesh is incorruptible
they say, then lie
immortal where the rest decays.

I am too slow a messenger
to speak her praise. For she
was proud and loyal and extravagant,
and her breast was pale as the dusky sky.

She'd roost aloft in the moon-browed elm
with the globe of midnight in her eye.

A Short Sad Ballad of the Fox

They took the fox in Brickyard Field
    And the green wheat sipped his blood.
The dogs unzipped him limb from limb
    And flayed him in the mud.

One remnant in a cart-rut
    Of the carcass that they dragged:
The foot that trod the midnight path
    Is a knot of sodden rag.

The cars that followed after
    Are turned and gone away
Like a funeral procession
    As the sun closed down the day.

Now the hunt is home and the moon is up
    And the stars are high and dark;
And across the hollows of the night
    The distant foxes bark.

Magpie

Magpie is nature's comic turn
trying to act straight.
Warden in uniform:
black shirt, white waistcoat,
hands behind back.

What's this?
A slug.
Very nice. Very nice.

And this?
Road Traffic Accident—
late out last night.

Soon deal with that.

Rats

The rat slips
like a bad thought,
guilty, hump-backed.
Just one today;
tomorrow dozens, families,
all making whoopee
in the sacks.

No choice but cat
and carcasses,
poison or trap.
At night
you whistle in the barn;
by day you clap
and the floor shucks.

Their sprung run's
sudden, sickening.
Each time you watch
another shape
insinuates
the drainpipe
where the blue bait's set.

No compromise.
They breed
like lessons in arithmetic.
In corners, dark, unconsciously,
big brothers thrive
on grievances,
and grow like debts.

Washing Line

For good we are sustained by images.
Slick advertisers know it and they give
Us back through their glass, their glossy pages
Transparent versions of all we approve.
What they exploit is our desire to live
Close to a sense, an ideal, of our selves
In sunlight where our kinder spirits move.

Take down the chosen packet from the shelf:
Each action says there's more at stake than chance.
By all we do we generate a wealth
Of pictures, the mind's bright hoard of icons,
Scenes from a magic book made to enhance
The memory of what's to come. Deceit
Or verity, the heart holds on to what it can.

And such is this, when I come round the house
To find you reaching in the rumpling sheets,
With the wind in your arms, the whole sky loose
Above you billowing, unfolding blue.
You have contrived its innocence complete:
Your pegs, your basket, all light's breathlessness;
Love's illustration, commonplace and true.

Dungarees

Two dungarees
on the washing-line
step-dancing
to the wind in time
like Okies
busking for a dime

or corpses
hanging from a tree—

splayed pockets
shrugging poverty

Green Man

(for Stan Hankins)

November, the word alone tolls,
sombre, slow on the tongue.
And no mere accident, I think,
that you should die in this
most closing month when the earth
draws in, draws self upon itself,
calls all its sap, its substance, down.

What's born in May (thorn's quick
spring syllable) utters its own end
in days like these, when hedges drip,
the small birds skulk from fork to fork,
and leaves that filter in their wrack
of twig, fall, mould themselves
to the ditch-bank's shape.

Hedge-seasons' grief. It schools
somewhere life roots, grips, waits again.
You said cut back the elm that fronts
our house, cut back its straggling
to the bone. Ah, Stan, you were
the last green man to tell us so!
I hear you laughing through the rain.

Elegy for an Old Carpet

When they began to cut them to the shapes
of rooms, carpets stopped travelling.
New carpets spread unblemished over cracks
and gaps, and bland as chat-show hosts
declare: This Is Your Future. Start Again.
The old ones coil their secrets, stains
and dark mottlings, pock-marks of chairs.
They hoard their spillages, and those
unfaded squares of time trapped under furniture;
and doggedly they still refuse to turn
to hide the paths our daily footsteps wear.

I shall be sorry when this one has gone,
the Wilton from an ancient aunt
we set our newly-wedded prospects on.
I like it when the morning sun
makes windows slowly and moves round,
and when in lamplight it becomes a ring
of ivies, blown leaves, whisperings.
Old carpets have their share in days
remembered and forgotten, cast away.
I sing their praise, their ends and beginnings:
all worn-out, baggy, threadbare things.

Aubade

I wake to music in the house:
one small boy playing, way below,
his fingers' trickle tickling sleep.
Another morning, and the rooms drift
back to shape and lap together
as the ship we're in
together checks its course.
Landfall of day. Another shore.
The floorboards shift; the boiler groans.
The sunlight rubs the grain
on well-loved furniture,
then blazes in the brass knob on the door.